Phong Nha, the Making of an American Smile

Tammy Nguyễn

for my uncle, Võ Văn Nhựt

In 1992, I found out that I was going to be missing two of my front teeth. I was eight, lying on the dentist's chair, staring at my velcro shoes when I heard Mrs. Nguyễn, the office administrator, cry: "We must help her!" My x-rays had just been processed, and they showed that my permanent lateral incisors did not exist. Just a week earlier, on the playground, I had been picking at my baby incisors, noodling my tongue around them and peeling them slowly away from my gums. They were the last of my baby teeth; I was getting excited for my permanent smile. But my excitement turned to confusion and anxiety upon learning that my smile would be abnormal.

Dr. Don rolled his chair over, x-rays in hand. "The teeth you just lost will not be replaced by new ones. Now, say: "O-O-O-O-O-O-O." He kept talking while he examined my mouth with his circular dental mirror. "We will have to figure out what to do with you. Some people let their teeth naturally fill in the empty spaces, so your canines would sit next to your front teeth. Others push the canines back to make room for false lateral incisors. We don't need these teeth anymore, and someday, no one will have them. You might be ahead of human evolution."

Four hundred million years ago, rain fell on Gondwana and eroded the limestone in the Earth. The Earth shifted. Wind pattered, slapped, and whipped, boring into the hollows of the rock, pushing the water ahead of it and sculpting the rock into an ecosystem of caves. Over millions of years, countless species thrived at the places where the meeting of acidic water and corrosive rock had created a matrix of riverways.

The Phong Nha Karst is located in the Annamite Mountains, which spread across the borders of Vietnam, Laos, and Cambodia. "Phong" is a Vietnamese word, derived from the Chinese word—"fung" in Cantonese or "feng" in Madarin—for "wind." "Nha" is Vietnamese for "teeth," though it is more commonly combined with other words to describe things related to teeth. For example, "Nha sĩ" means dentist; "Nha khoa" means "dentistry." According to Chinese mythology, the Phong Nha Karst is the Earth's teeth, carved by wind.

In 1992, Vietnam adopted a new constitution. After the fall of the Soviet Union, the country sought to become more viable in the global economy; the new constitution allowed for more foreign investment and ownership.

In this same year a former farmer, Yang Guoqiang, opened his company Country Garden—a real estate developer that, decades later, would change the shape of land in Asia.

As Mr. Guoqiang started to grow his company in '92, another farmer named Hồ Khanh, who lived in the Phong Nha Mountains, wanted to hide away from the rain. He found a hole and crawled in, only to find that the hole was endless, so he kept going.

My uncle was born Võ Văn Nhựt. It was agreed by everyone in the Chợ Cây Quéo neighborhood of Sài Gòn that he was the most handsome man in the area. He was tall, broad-shouldered, kept a muscular physique, and carried himself with a macho confidence. The beauty people saw in him he also demanded of others; he associated beauty with wealth, and wealth with success. He expected people to have high noses, fit body frames—and, his biggest fixation, a straight and glowing smile.

In the 1960s my uncle was a pilot for the South Vietnamese Air Force, and they sent him to Texas to train. This might have been when he decided that America possessed the most beauty, wealth, and success of any country on Earth. He became a successful businessman in the '70s, after he was released from duty. Seeded with Western ambition, he began exporting Vietnamese porcelain for a company with an office in Florida. Back and forth he went, pushing empty vessels from Vietnam in the land of dreams. He pushed so many vessels that he was able to build one for himself, in the form of a giant French-style house for his mother and ten siblings.

Three years later, when he was traveling with a fleet of empty vessels from Vietnam to Florida, he decided to escape westward, from Florida's balmy beaches to the arid desert of Reno, Nevada. Under a sublime sun, the Sierra Nevada Mountains infused him with a motivation he had never felt before. Sporting a tough, squeaky leather jacket in his Chevrolet Chevelle, he cruised the wide highways of Nevada, looking for a permanent path in America.

It didn't take long for him to map his road by way of a Vietnamese woman, already a US citizen, named Maria. My uncle married her, and together they ran a nail salon in Reno, tending to the aesthetic aspirations of women, and their appetite for the casino scene. It must have been around this time that he changed his name to David Van—David was for David who fought Goliath, and Van, extracted from his real middle name, was meant to make his new American name sound a little Dutch.

By 1980, the nail salon had become tiresome and the marriage had lost its luster, so David Van bundled all of his savings to score a taxi medallion in San Francisco. That piece of metal would soon make him millions. He leased it out to other drivers at inflated rates that started to earn him a reputation, particularly among the Vietnamese drivers: my uncle was a crooked dude.

Despite my father's hesitation about David Van, my mother loved him, and he became part of my daily life around 1992, when his life collapsed. By then he had three ex-wives, an abandoned business with the first, a disowned child from the second, and two more kids who left with their mother from the third.

Alone, he started to come to our house for dinner several times a week. He would tell long yarns about this person and that person, pounding his fist passionately on my parents' oak dining table. He'd be wearing a short-sleeved polo shirt, his left tricep flexing beneath it when his clenched hand hit the surface of the table. Seated directly across from him, I would see David Van's gorgeous American eagle tattoo, which wrapped around his upper arm. It was an image of the fierce bird of prey with its wings slightly spread upward. Both of its claws clutched the pole of an American flag as the banner waved behind its body. The ink of the tattoo had blended and faded to a peaceful greenish-grey color. It really seemed to be a part of my uncle's skin; as his tricep pulsed, the eagle and the American flag breathed with it.

After dinner, my parents and David Van stayed up for hours watching *Paris by Night* videos. In these highly-produced concerts, Vietnamese entertainers of the war diaspora would sing and dance to traditional music and contemporary pop tunes. Sitting back in the recliner with a grin on his face, still clenching his fists, my uncle would point out which performers had veneers, which had implants, and which had natural teeth. His own smile was perfect and, I always assumed, natural (later, my father told me that my uncle's perfect smile, just like his nose and eyelids, was fake). "Teeth are everything," David Van advised my parents. "The Americans take you seriously when you have a nice set of teeth. It doesn't matter how smart you are—if you have a good face with nice, straight white teeth, people will take you seriously in this country. You'd better take her to see the orthodontist."

My orthodontist, Dr. Tinloy, had an office across the street from Dr. Don's on Van Ness. The glory of the American Dream could be traced along this famous street, starting from its southernmost tip. There, you found San Francisco's cultural institutions: Davis Symphony Hall, the Asian Art Museum, and the Main Library. Moving north, the Civic Center gave way to UC Berkeley's Hastings Law School campus, followed by clothing boutiques, movie theaters, car dealerships, steak houses, and office buildings, until, finally, you reached the Russian Hill neighborhood—one of the wealthiest areas of San Francisco, full of Victorian townhouses with views of the Golden Gate Bridge.

Insurance wouldn't cover the cost of the braces. After seeing the bill, my dad looked up at Dr. Tinloy and asked, "Is this necessary?" "It's entirely cosmetic," the doctor replied. My dad hesitated, then nodded and took out his credit card. A week later, I got my braces.

The appointment took two hours. First, they cleaned my teeth, then they covered them with a glue that smelled awful, like nail polish. Next, a variety of metal parts were secured to the adhesive. My molars were fitted with hooked metal frames that encircled each tooth like a corset.

The reason these metal squares had this particular, tiled configuration on top of them was because braces technology depends on an interaction between a wire strung across your teeth and your teeth's movements. The wire would be fed through all the metal mechanisms and then be secured to the hooks on the back molars with rubber bands. If some teeth needed to be pushed apart, springs could be beaded onto the wire, putting pressure on the metal squares which would then push your teeth apart over the course of a few weeks. And if you needed to pull teeth closer together, they could attach a rubber band to the metal pieces that had a hook.

There were two treatment plans for someone with my birth defect. One path was to close the spaces created by the absence of the lateral incisors. The canines would tightly sit next to the front teeth and be reshaped to blend into the smile—it would look like something was still missing but you couldn't figure out what. The other path was to push the canines away from the front teeth to create space for prosthetic incisors. Anyone with any foresight (my dentist, my orthodontist, and parents) knew that a path leading to permanent prosthetics would be more time consuming and exponentially more costly. My protocol would be the first one, to close up the gaps.

The day after I got my braces was exciting, and painful. I couldn't eat anything, not even the recommended treat of ice cream. I remember that phở noodles were the easiest thing to eat, especially when they'd been soaked in my mother's broth; if I cut up the noodles, I could slurp them into my throat and bypass chewing altogether. By the third week, I was back to normal. The metal on my teeth had become part of my body. My lips couldn't remember a time when the surface of my teeth was smooth. By the third week, I was also doing all the things you weren't supposed to do, like eating popcorn and chewing gum.

On my first routine visit to the orthodontist, Dr. Tinloy made a consequential decision in a matter of seconds. He noticed that if my teeth were to continue moving along the trajectory they'd started, I would eventually lose my ability to bite. Without explaining to me why, he changed my protocol and started using the braces to push my teeth apart.

Over the course of five years, Dr. Tinloy pushed my canines away from my two front teeth using a sequence of springs: one sixteenth of an inch, then an eighth, then three sixteenths, then a quarter, and on and on until the springs were half an inch long. Springs became a signature feature of my smile throughout middle school and into the 11th grade.

The thing about having missing front teeth is that it is worse than having ugly teeth. Having missing front teeth is more than a merely deformed smile. To David Van and my parents, this meant that you were poor and uneducated, and I believed this too. I'm not sure if anyone noticed that two giant openings were being created in my mouth, but I know I found solace in my "mouth full of metal." It kept me from being a girl who was missing two front teeth.

In my five years of having braces, no one mentioned looks. No one talked to me about beauty. Instead, they talked to me about my bite. The stated goal of any orthodontic treatment was to have a good bite, one where your upper teeth and lower teeth lined up correctly as "nature intended." In a proper bite, front teeth slightly overlap, and bottom molars act like the negative mold of the upper molars; there aren't any awkward meeting points between your teeth that would create a risk of grinding. The other reason people gave for getting braces was hygiene: less food gets stuck in a mouth of straight teeth, making them easier to clean.

But I didn't have crooked teeth. I had spaced-out teeth; I barely needed to floss. I didn't grind my teeth either. My bite was fine.

My husband and I met our tour group in Quảng Bình Province, the region of Vietnam through which the Phong Nha Karst weaves. I was immediately awestruck by the sight of the mountains in the distance. Miles of rice paddies surrounded them like a carpet, or a grand driveway, or a gigantic lawn meant to emphasize the importance of a place. The rice paddies glistened electric green, a shade you might see at a nightclub or painted on a Lamborghini. It was strange to see such a green in nature.

Our group consisted of a German family of four and a young Dutch couple who were both dentists. Our guide, Đông, had lived in the Quảng Bình his whole life. On the drive over to the Oxalis Adventure office, Đông gave us a friendly brief about the region. "A long time ago," he said, "the whole region was water, and you can tell which caves are younger because water still runs through them."

We had to walk 45 minutes to get to the mouth of the first cave. As we entered the forest from a flat dirt road, the landscape turned immediately picturesque. In the distance, the mountains waited peacefully for us, covered in foliage like dense, curly hair. A stream appeared where some buffalo were drinking water; a few young ones tailed their mothers and others grazed at the grass. As we kept walking we came across some large dirt platforms. "This is how the village people bury their dead," explained Đông. "After the body decomposes, the remaining bones get transferred across the road, where the other family members are buried."

"This is also the home of King Kong," Đông continued. In 2016, Warner Brothers, Legendary Entertainment, and Tencent Productions brought part of the $185-million dollar *Kong Skull Island* production to Quảng Bình. They set King Kong's birthplace in the exact area we were passing. "They shut down this whole area for weeks," said Đông. In a video posted online, the director, Jordan Vogt-Roberts, can be heard praising the region's beauty over a soundtrack of Hollywood adventure music. "I kept asking, do people understand how beautiful this is?" he asked. "To me, it's so otherworldly and spectacular, and it's just the daily life of other people. I hope that they realize how special the place that they live in is."

Đông continued to educate our group. "Our village didn't get electricity until 2003. Before tourism, life was hard. Many people were hunters and gatherers, using hand weapons and oil lamps to gather food and to make a living. You could eat anything you found in the forest. Most of our meals were wild birds, rats, and small gophers. We have more opportunities now with more people coming to visit." The grass got taller until we were walking amidst human-sized shrubbery. We reached another stream and submerged ourselves, entering the water up to our waists to cross.

There were two porters who followed our group, carrying our jugs of water and snacks: bananas; packs of Oreos in strawberry, original, and blueberry flavors; and rice crackers. The porters also helped us to get over difficult crossings, where it got steep or thick with shrubs. As we moved along, one of the porters started to sing a Vietnamese country song. I didn't know the song, but I have deep childhood memories of the style: my grandmother would play similar songs, loud, from VHS recordings brought over from Vietnam.

"O-O-O-O-O-O-O!" The porter's lone voice bellowed around us. These songs often feature a bird, a fish, a river, a longing for a past time, usually a lover. The melodies are melancholic, each long note slurring into the next, never a bright interval. They almost always end in a fadeaway. Wherever I hear these songs—at my parents' home through their booming karaoke system or here in the jungles of Vietnam—I can feel the structure of the melody sculpt itself into the physical world. Each word ricochets off whatever surface it can find—be it a living room couch, rock, chair, or leaf—and molds its sadness onto my surroundings.

"These must have been the same songs that were sung in war," I thought to myself. We were not just walking along an adventure trail to a geological wonder; these jungles were part of the Hồ Chí Minh Trail. I asked Đông where exactly the trail was. "It was everywhere," he said, his hands gesturing all around him. "If not for the Hồ Chí Minh Trail, we would have lost our country."

Also known as the Trường Sơn Trail, the Hồ Chí Minh Trail was not a trail in the sense of a path that connects point A to point B. It was a changing, breathing organism: a network of dirt roads, much like the one my group and I were trekking on, that started in the south of Hà Nội in Northern Vietnam then moved southwest into eastern Laos and Cambodia, through the Annamite

Mountain Range, where the Phong Nha Karst lies. Through mountains and jungle, the trail continued southward into eastern Cambodia and terminated in South Vietnam, west of Đà Lạt. Many people credit this network, which was the conduit for humans and supplies moving from the North to the South, as the reason for the Northern Vietnamese victory in the American War.

Use of the trail began in 1959. The US Navy had blocked the coastline, so the Northern Vietnamese army needed to find a way to transport supplies to the south. Colonel Võ Bẩm of the People's Army of Vietnam was assigned to the task. He was a soldier who had fought in the anti-French war in the Annamite Mountains from 1946-1954. He recalled that the Việt Minh (anti-French) leaders had created a supply line, the "Reunification Trail," that ran through Vietnam's Central Highlands. The colonel hypothesized that if there could be a similar trail allowing for weapons to be handed off at stations farther south, and if several trips could be made over the course of a year, the South had a chance to be unified with the North.

The soldiers who circuited the trail were called Hà Nội's 559th Transportation Group, and by 1961, there were about 2,000 of them. Their force was amplified by thousands of volunteers—many of them teenagers and women—who helped make the network fluid. The heart of this system was the porters, and arguably everyone was a kind of a porter: each person had some kind of a vessel—rucksack, shovel, box, bicycle, truck—that could carry weapons and food to their brothers and sisters in the South.

The United States knew that they needed to eliminate this network in order to win the war, and they tried. Three million tons of explosives were dropped. That's a million more than were dropped on Germany and Japan combined in all of WWII. Chemical defoliants, including Agent Orange, were also sprayed, destroying thousands of acres of jungle. But the People's Army of

Vietnam had control of the ground; they kept moving. For each crater created by a bomb, teams of volunteers with shovels would fill in the hole. Sometimes they would set traps, tricking the US Air Force into blowing up the side of a mountain so that they could use the gravel that resulted from the explosion.

The trail became the site of daily life for the people who kept the network alive. Songs were sung, pictures were drawn, diaries were written, and plenty of alcohol and smoke were passed around between comrades for the cause. While many Vietnamese people on the trail died as a result of bombings, even more succumbed to environmental hazards. Thousands died from heat exhaustion, fever, and snake bites.

The snakes that didn't bite were killed and eaten, along with gophers and other rodents, over salty rice cooked on open fires.

In the summer of 2000, I was fifteen and got my braces off, along with my first pair of false teeth. For one week, as I waited for the prosthetic to be made, the gaps in my mouth would be exposed. I knew I was lucky that this happened while school was on break and no one would see.

I hid at home for that week. I remember the strange sensation of running my tongue along my bare gums. I had difficulty speaking, specifically enunciating "s" sounds. On the day of my fitting, the retainer was waiting for me on a silver tray at Dr. Tinloy's office. It was a dainty thing, a transparent pink piece of plastic with two false teeth attached to it by a thin bridge of more pink plastic. When Dr. Tinloy slipped it in my mouth, it didn't look right: there were huge spaces between the prosthetic teeth and my gums. My heart raced. Dr. Tinloy took out the retainer and carved away at the plastic with his Dremel drill. The adjustments were tedious, but after ten or fifteen rounds of carving, re-inserting, and repeating, something sort of worked. The retainer fit, and the teeth looked acceptable.

As I left with my dad, Dr. Tinloy cautioned, "I wouldn't eat with that thing in your mouth, the teeth are much too fragile." I knew already that I wouldn't listen to that rule. What was I going to do, let the world know I was missing two of my front teeth?

That day, we went to Great America and rode the Vortex—the rollercoaster where you stand up. David Van had convinced my mother that thrill-seeking entertainment was good for one's blood pressure, that it served to "shake things up" and "even everything out." Riding the roller coasters at Great America became a bi-weekly weekend excursion, for the sake of our health.

When I had braces, the wind ran through the gaps of my teeth like big swooshes of ice. But that day, with my new prosthetics, I was so terrified my fake teeth would fly out of my mouth that I clenched my jaw the whole time, waiting for the ride to end. The fear of losing my teeth would follow me for the next nineteen years of my life.

All that I feared happened. Once, my mom accidentally threw out my false teeth while I was brushing my real teeth. Another time, I bit on a straw and the whole right false tooth broke off. I held it together with a piece of chewing gum and ran from school all the way to the dentist's. Another time, I walked into Dr. Don's office for a checkup and regrettably told him that I needed him to look at my prosthetic because I was holding it together with super glue. He ended up snipping off a piece of a paper clip and placing it inside of a hole he dug out of my retainer. Once, in college, I was on a date eating nachos and both of my false teeth broke off. I ran to a bodega, pretending to buy beers for later, and got superglue, which I used to stick my teeth back to the retainer in the taco-bar bathroom. I don't think many people—if any—knew about my situation, unless I told them.

One year, David Van and my mom decided that we would all go to Kauai. This was typical; they shared an obsession with health and a fear of dying, coupled with a fixation on wealth, that compelled them to plan frequent excursions "for our health"—always in aspirational, exotic locales. My family did not skimp on accommodations when we traveled. On this trip, we stayed at a "gold-crown" resort that was part of a timeshare my parents and David Van owned. The beachfront suite was large enough to sleep all seven of us: my mom, my dad, my sister, David Van, his two kids, and me.

We learned that Kauai was where *Jurassic Park* was filmed and that there was an action-packed, mountain-Jeep adventure that would take us on a tour of the locations. It was a cloudy, muggy day when the Jeep, decked out with *Jurassic Park* decals, pulled up to our resort. I remember David Van hanging onto one of the Jeep's straps, his eagle tattoo throbbing with his muscles as he laughed. We splashed through pool after pool of mud, and brown water flicked onto our faces and clothes as my cousins and I giggled in delight. Seven hours flew by.

The rest of our vacation was filled with beach play and long drives all over the island to visit new properties. On these vacations, David Van and my parents enjoyed pretending to be real estate investors. They would seek out a local agent and inquire about a new development with such commitment that I wasn't always sure if they were pretending. David Van would drive all seven of us in a rented minivan, for hours sometimes, until we'd reach a mostly vacant lot of land, the site of some new development that would be finished within the next five to ten years. There was always one model unit that was furnished and decorated as a sales pitch. There was nothing special about the development in Kauai. The walls were white; the unit was air-conditioned; there was a place to grill, a place to park, and a bathtub off of the master bedroom. You could choose a studio, one-bedroom, two-bedroom, or three-bedroom.

After visiting one of the empty model homes, the agent would take us out to lunch: salad, a steak or burger, fruit, maybe ice cream. In the car ride back, my parents and David Van would debrief, my uncle taking most of the airtime with his passionate exclamations. For emphasis, he might gather his fists and pound them on the steering wheel. They would talk about how much you'd need to rent the unit for to make a profit, how much property taxes were, and, bottom line, how much better off they were with the properties they had already bought in the Bay Area.

After the long day, my cousins and I were always rewarded with more beach or pool play and a lavish dinner at an all-you-can-eat buffet, where my dad would caution me in front of everyone to be careful with my teeth.

This sequence of vacation events repeated over the next several years: thrill-seeking entertainment, real estate touring, then pool or beach, and an all-you-can-eat buffet. The same conversations and topics would be brought up. In Florida we went to all of the theme parks of Disney World and drove all over Orlando looking for new houses to not buy. In Vegas, we went through all of the water amusements and then went out into the desert looking for smart investments. In my years with braces, I only had to be careful at the buffets. But after I received my prosthetic, there would be times when I had to take out my false teeth at dinner. There was a constant anxiety that my prosthetic teeth would break off in the middle of one of these vacations, and I would be toothless in a situation where we needed to look wealthy and educated.

"It is impossible to count the number of species of plants in Phong Nha," Đông told the group as we continued to pry our way through the jungle. Each corner of my vision was oozing with life, but a kind of life that wasn't nice, welcoming, or virtuous. Here, the jungle fluttered with a density of leaves in tiny, small, large, and enormous sizes. A palm branch stuck out from its tree, though I could not see its tree. Each leaf of the palm extruded from the stem like a long, narrow dagger. Vines twirled around like venomous snakes. Another branch with an abundance of tongue-shaped leaves collected water. Long grasses stuck out from every dark crevice like pieces of dried hair. Star fruits hung from above like sleeping bats, and tamarind pods hung from other branches, pregnant with seeds. The jungle lured you with its beauty, flirting with your temptations. While some plants were medicinal and many could be eaten, there were others that could make you itch and some that could kill you. It was a morality-free terrain.

After we crawled through the thicket of jungle, the opening of another cave appeared. "Before the British came, people lived in the caves, but they did not go in very far. The Vietnamese people are deeply superstitious, even here in Quảng Bình, which is mostly Catholic. They tell stories about ghosts waiting in the caves to catch you." The opening of this cave reminded me of an empty nativity manger. We climbed up to the entrance and saw the cave slope downward then open to a spacious flat area. The porters got there before us and created a beautiful spread of the bananas, water, and Oreos they'd carried for us on the laborious trek. We ate and drank, doused our faces with water, and took selfies until it was time to go inside.

As our group descended downward, tooth-like cones the size of Greek columns started to appear; soon, they were everywhere. They looked like draped Christian statues that had lost their faces: a candidate for the Virgin Mary hovered over us. Our headlights animated the cones; it seemed as if the statues were looking at us. I was in church; the cave's hollow seemed to possess a sermon. My bones ached, and the sweat on my face stung as it mixed with the dust from the hike.

Above our heads, cones of geological rock hung like dripping candle wax. There was a shimmer from the cave matter: tiny planes of limestone, salt, and gypsum glittered in silver and gold. Around us, boulders stacked like ancient books of knowledge. The ground below was a mixture of rock, sand, and shell-like shards. It was as if we were standing on the diseased tongue of a mouth overgrown with teeth.

When I looked back to the cave's opening, it looked like the sun: a big round disc hitting the cave rock with its bright good light.

One of the porters whistled and gestured at us to come over. He pointed to the side of a large rock wall: "Fossil."

Buried within the rock was something that looked a bit like a snail, its spiral shell interwoven with geological layers. It glistened under our headlights, luminescent white and rust. The air was so dry in this old cave that it exaggerated our breath and sweat, the only places where moisture was excreted. The organisms around us had been dead for millions of years, but we were very much alive.

We continued to criss-cross the cave aimlessly until the exit hole showed its bright light, as if to say "come here." It was so bright it hurt. I squinted so the light could rest on my eyelashes. My eyelids slowly opened, gradually letting in bits of light.

In 2007, 22 years old and a recent college grad, I moved to Sài Gòn. In my mouth was my fourth pair of prosthetic teeth.

David Van would call me every so often, just to say hello, and I enjoyed talking to him as I drove around the fast-developing city. He would tell me that I reminded him of himself when he was young and running around Sài Gòn. He'd ask if I'd kept up my blog and told me how much he liked seeing my pictures and reading my stories. There were two things he would usually ask me to do for him. One was to go to Citibank to take out some money he'd transferred to me to give to my grandmother's caretakers. The other was to drive by Saigon Pearl, a new real estate development where he had recently made a big down payment.

I did both. I lived in an industrial part of town, and I would drive my motorbike to the center to stop at Citibank, then loop over to Saigon Pearl, and then to my aunt's house to give her the money so she could pass it to the caretaker.

There was almost never anything to see at Saigon Pearl. The development occupied a long stretch of road, maybe 400 meters, but it was boarded up with a grey-green aluminum fence on which blue letters spelled out "Saigon Pearl." Elsewhere, a billboard displayed renderings of apartments overlooking the Sài Gòn River. Somewhere, a slogan declared "Luxury Saigon." But you could tell that, behind the fence, there was nothing but a pile of dirt and a couple of cranes.

Two years later, when I was 24 and still living in Sài Gòn, David Van died suddenly. Everyone was shocked that someone so big, strong, and beautiful could die so abruptly. The police found his rotting corpse alone in his bed after they responded to a call that there was a foul smell secreting from his house. The cause of death was a heart attack.

Not long after his death, I was at a business meeting, trying to score a commission for myself and some friends to paint a mural at a cafe that was still under construction. There I was, pitching a wall painting of abstract trees and changing seasons and sipping an iced coffee. There was plenty of small talk and laughter as we chatted about colors and how to make the trees look like a Vietnamese forest and to make the cafe look expensive. Then I bit on a piece of ice that snapped my right false tooth off. Panicking inside but still maintaining a networking-cool, I navigated the meeting to a "let's keep talking" conclusion. Before I got on my bike, I called an uncle of mine whose wife was a dentist. Without telling him why, I asked if I could see her right away.

I zipped through the city to get to her office, passing by the Saigon Pearl development on the way. Something had changed there. A high grey tower had been built. There were no windows yet, but way up high in the sky a crane seemed to be in the process of adding more floors.

"Water!" Đông said, pointing at the ground. A stream ran across our path. "This water runs into the ground, through the cave, and out the other side. We will see this water again inside and swim through it," he explained. We were entering another cave. This one had undisturbed walls striped in soft graduated watermarks extending horizontally into the cave. Smooth cavities ran along the walls. I felt the presence of water; it was much cooler even just a few feet into the opening. As we walked deeper in, the light disappeared, and our headlights became our shiny, frantic, guiding stars.

Small black bats circled around us, unafraid. Their wings made a pleasant whipping sound. Then there was a steep drop, which we had to climb down using a long ladder. Each of us in the group went down, one by one. Towards the bottom, we could hear the sound of running water. We migrated towards the sound, passing by smooth, water-stained cave rocks. I could feel the ground soften. A bright blue fluttering movement landed on a rock. It was a common bluebottle butterfly, a well-known species in the Phong Nha Karst. The blue of its wings was so bright next to the browns, greys, and whites, it might have come down from the sun.

The sound of the water was still roaring, but it came from a place we could not see. "Go," said the porter, who was already at the edge. One by one, we entered the water and started to swim. Cave rocks protruded beneath the water, and we had to use our feet as eyes, treading water tentatively in order to safely advance. The passageway became narrower until we were traversing a corridor just two feet wide. The cave walls tapered above our heads like the ceilings of old gothic cathedrals. "Now turn off your headlights," instructed Đông, "and follow the sound of my voice." We turned off our lights. It was darker than black. I opened my eyes as wide as I could, hoping to see a slight shadow through the darkness, but there was nothing.

"O-O-O-O-O-O-O," Đông started to sing himself. "Try to follow my voice, okay? O-O-O-O-O-O-O." I started to inch toward the sound. Below me, the cave floor continued to protrude: sharp cones, bumpy boulders, round mounds. My hands were pushed up against the cave walls to help me navigate through the water. "O-O-O-O-O-O-O," Đông continued to call us forward.

The first sign of light emerged from above as a long, skinny triangle that traced a cavern shard hanging from the ceiling. It was the faintest blue color. Then, another long, angular shape appeared, and another, and another. There was something about seeing light again that felt like salvation. My hearing was directional in a way it had never been before. The faint blue light, though easier on the eyes than walking back into the sun, was a reminder of how dark it had just been, and also of how powerful listening could be.

"O-O-O-O-O-O-O!" As the waterway opened into a wider, river-like path, Đông swam ahead; his sound began to transform into a country song. We could now see the light from the cave's exit reflecting on the water. Each triangular current of water started to glisten with yellow until the entire stream became a tessellation of yellow diamonds reflecting the strengthening light. Framed by the contours of the cave mouth, Đông had become a black shape rimmed with sunbeams.

We swam into a secluded pond in the middle of the mountains. It was completely surrounded by castle-high rocks and jungle. We couldn't see anything outside; no one would ever find us here. As we swam out, the sun kissed our wet faces. We could smell food roasting on hot coals. As we emerged from the water, we were greeted with a wholesome spread of tropical fruit and sweet biscuits. The porters were there already, cooking for us; clay pots of rice and jugs of tea were brought out as we gathered around.

"Did the early cave dwellers ever make pots out of the mud from the cave?" I asked Đông. "Yes!" Đông said excitedly, "You can sometimes see their ceramic remains in the rocks. You can tell that people really lived there." A porter brought out a bowl of herbs. It was time to eat.

My husband and I sat with the Dutch dentist couple. Our lunch was grilled pork and omelettes wrapped with rice crepes and dressed with an assortment of herbs and *cheo* ("jungle sauce"), a dipping concoction unique to the Quảng Bình region. The flavor of the *cheo* was delicious and overwhelming; it framed the common flavors of the rest of the ingredients and made them belong to this place. Taste sensations floated around my mouth and around my new implants, exciting the nerves along my gums.

"How long have you guys been dentists?" I asked the Dutch couple.

"Well, actually, I'm a dentist, but he is in school for oral surgery," the woman said.

"Oh wow, I just got implants!" I was excited.

"Oh really? Which ones?" the man asked.

"My lateral incisors."

The two of them smiled in acknowledgment. "Very common, very common," they both nodded.

"They look great," the woman said.

"Thank you," I replied.

"It is very expensive to do that in America, no?" the woman asked.

My husband and I both laughed, nodding our heads yes. "And it took forever," I said, "how much is it for one in the Netherlands?"

"So little, so little compared to America, maybe $700 US dollars," said the man. "But nothing is as good as in America." The woman laughed in agreement. "America has the best dental technology. Nothing beats the American smile."

I had been a patient of Dr. Neal Fujishige for a few years when I told him that I finally wanted to undergo the procedure. I asked for a cost estimate; I knew that permanent implants would be expensive, and insurance was unlikely to cover much, if any, of the cost, because it is considered cosmetic surgery. The estimate came back: $15,000. I swallowed, thought of David Van and the American smile.

Think of an implant like a screw in a wall. The longer the screw, the more secure it will be and the more weight it can carry. A successful implant needs at least 10mm of space going up into the gums in order to provide a strong hold. In cases like mine, while the gaps where the lateral incisors should be appear large, there usually isn't enough room between the bones of the front teeth and those of the canines for an implant to fit.

The precision of the angle is also important, because the area is extremely close to the sinuses—part of the respiratory system connected to the nose and throat. If the angle of the implant is off, permanent nerve damage could result. And Dr. Fujishige was concerned about aesthetics: "It needs to be perfect, it needs to be perfect," he told me again and again. Since the lateral incisors are so visible, Dr. Fujishige was adamant that they look seamless—as if I were born with them.

I was prescribed six months of Invisalign for another $5,500. Dr. Fujishige's goal was to get the bones of my front teeth and canines to move as far away from each other as possible.

My concern, as always, was to not let anyone see that I was missing teeth.

The fitted, clear-plastic Invisalign molds required another level of creative eating. I had gotten used to my prosthetics—I'd been wearing them for eighteen years. I knew to bite a carrot using only my front teeth. I would cut steak into pieces small enough to use only my molars to chew. I never bit into whole apples. Aligners were different—most people take them off during meals. But for me, that would mean excusing myself to a bathroom, removing them without letting my fake teeth fall out (into a toilet), and re-inserting my prosthetic—then reversing the steps twenty minutes later, once lunch was over.

After two months and four aligners, Dr. Fujishige was disappointed in the lack of bone movement. He adjusted the procedure, giving me a whole new set of aligners, this time with "attachments." In aligner-speak, attachments are tooth-colored pieces of plastic that are fused to the surfaces of your teeth to provide additional traction as the aligners pull your bones into their new shape. Now, my front teeth and canines all had plastic fused to them. It was almost like having braces again.

Forest City is a man-made island located in the Johor Strait, two kilometers away from Singapore and another two kilometers from mainland Malaysia. Its construction began in 2015. Its developer, Country Garden, one of the most powerful Chinese real estate companies, partnered with Sultan Ibrahim, the Sultan of the Malaysian state Johor, for the project. This man-made island has been called a present-day Atlantis and claims to be the world's foremost sustainable city. It runs solely on renewable energy and is able to absorb 10,000 tons of carbon from the air annually. When Forest City is completed, it will be covered in greenery: nearly one million plants, made up of more than 100 species and 40,000 individual trees. This utopia on the water is also completely tax free.

I contacted Forest City's sales office and told them I was a professor and artist in New York City with frequent business in Asia. I was going to be having an exhibition of my paintings in Hồ Chí Minh City in August of 2019 and would like to visit Forest City with the prospect of purchasing an investment property. A man named Alston Aw responded to me on Whatsapp. I had reached out to him a year before my exhibition, and throughout that year he sent me copious amounts of well-designed informational material about Forest City—as well as Christmas, New Year, and Lunar New Year greetings.

I flew to Johor from Hồ Chí Minh City on the morning of August 4, 2019. Mr. Aw picked me up in a silver Toyota. He was a soft-spoken man, but he didn't waste any time explaining my itinerary. Forest City was about 30 minutes away from the Johor International Airport. I was being taken to a welcome lunch; I would then tour all of the properties, concluding with the resort next to the new golf course where the developer had gifted me a one-night stay in the King Suite.

The highway in Johor was clean and lined with trees. After a large onramp, Forest City rose from the horizon. A giant billboard covered in shrubbery read, *"FOREST CITY."* A collection of identical white towers grew higher and higher as we drove closer. To my right-hand side, a big complex that looked like a convention center appeared, with impressive metal lettering across its roof: *"SHATTUCK-ST. MARY'S FOREST CITY INTERNATIONAL*

SCHOOL." Not many cars were going our way, but the ghostly city shimmered with excitement. A security booth greeted us upon arrival. As they inspected his ID, Mr. Aw smiled at me and said, "They always want to know who is here because everything is tax free. First lunch, okay?" I nodded.

We parked in an underground parking lot and took an elevator up to what looked like a high-tech contemporary mall. Well-lit, air-conditioned, glass windows from floor to ceiling, white marble floors, zig-zagging escalators leading to glistening places, and fake plants everywhere: they splayed over the balconies and erupted in potted arrangements every few feet. There was even a string of plastic leaves wrapped around the cord of the hand-drying machine in the bathroom.

The dining area was vast and dim. The buffet itself was spotlit, resembling an oval stage starring international cuisine: giant prawns drenched in a coconut peanut sauce, sautéed cabbage, pasta with multiple sauces, curry stewed chicken, stir-fried beef, rice, a variety of pickled vegetables, and a fountain of Sprite. There was hardly anyone there, just a trio of chatty Hà-Nội-an women and a young Chinese family in a far, lonely corner. I had a little of everything, and so did Mr. Aw. He told me how clean everything is in Forest City, unlike Vietnam; that it's a great place for kids; that, because all the cars are underground, there's no pollution above. There are great schools, in case my kids want to get into Harvard. And it's a wonderful place for old people because of Malaysia's mild tropical climate.

After lunch, we went up another level on the escalator, and right as we got off there was an enormous twinkling model of Forest City. The floors of different complexes blinked in an alternating pattern to give the appearance of a bustling paradise. Restaurants were lit with blue and magenta LEDs; boats and yachts were glued to an ultra-blue resin pour standing in for the water. Giant signs read "Commercial Street" and "Transportation Hub." We were greeted by another man, a sales representative for the Forest City luxury apartments. A jovial man with a "smiling with your eyes" face.

Behind a wall covered in plastic plants was an enormous diorama which diagrammed the history and vision of Forest City. A label read *"STRATEGIC LOCATION."* Below that, a giant green plexiglass map of the world showed Forest City's centrality to a whole network of countries and cities, with thin blue lines uniting them under the One Belt, One Road vision: Singapore, Malaysia, Indonesia, Brunei, Philippines, Haikou, Sanzhou, Xi'an, Lanzhou, Urumqi, Khorgas, Kazakhstan, Kyrgyzstan, Tajikistan, Uzbekistan, Iran, Sri Lanka, India, Turkey, Russia, Kenya, Greece, Italy, Germany, and Holland.

The Smiling Salesman gestured at another model, a big cross-section of the man-made land mass with a blinking line indicating the different stages of the process. Lots of places have been made from reclaimed land, he said, like Palm Islands in Dubai, and Changi Airport in Singapore. "Reclaimed land technology is very advanced," he said, pointing to the three layers of earth in the model: rock, soil, sand. The rock and soil are found on-site, but the sand is brought in from elsewhere to create the land mass, hence the term "reclaimed land." You can only create reclaimed land where the sea is not very deep. Here in Forest City, the sea is just two to six meters deep. "It's been built to its maximum size."

As the Smiling Salesman told me this, I thought about what I'd been reading, about the cost of this imported sand. I had learned that small islands not far from Forest City, in the Riau Islands of Indonesia, had disappeared overnight. Their sand was loaded onto ships, which sailed off into Singaporean waters, just 20 minutes away by commuter ferry.

After the land is compressed, concrete and steel pipes are drilled thirty to forty meters deep through the sand, soil, and rock. This infrastructure gives the man-made land its strength. All of the buildings that make up Forest City were designed and manufactured at the industrial park within the nearby special economic zone. After the land was ready, the parts were driven over the bridge and assembled with cranes.

Below the land-building model was a quote that read: *With blue skies, white clouds, pure sea breeze and haze-free air all year round, it is the most livable country in Asia.* And beneath that, five green illuminated discs read: *Tropical climate, 21°C - 32°C, PM 2.5 = excellent, UV index comfortable 5-8.*

"No climate change here," the Smiling Salesman said.

"When can we get moving on this?" I asked Dr. Fujishige.

Dr. Fujishige wanted me to have the best surgeon in New York City, someone who would be as meticulous as he was. After an unsuccessful phone consultation with a Canadian in Midtown Manhattan, he forwarded me to Dr. Harrison Chen, another Midtown oral surgeon. Dr. Chen could not have been more than 40 years old. He was very kind, with an extremely strong handshake that reminded me of David Van. He was fit, built like some of the porters in the Phong Nha Karst. His confidence was intimidating. Our consultation took about thirty minutes; twenty minutes in the waiting room and, at most, ten with him. After he shook my hand, he took a quick glance at the screen, then turned to me. "Say O-O-O-O-O-O-O." With his circular dental mirror, he examined my mouth. "I can do this, I can work with this."

"That's it?" I asked. "Why has everyone, my entire life, made such a big deal out of this surgery?"

"I can do this," Dr. Chen said.

A week later, after Dr. Fujishige had given it the green light, the operation was booked for July 12th, 2018.

The Smiling Salesman took me to another wall with a giant map of the Iskandar Special Economic Zone. Guided by his laser pointer, I learned that the Zone exists because of Singapore; that Singapore is a small country—only 719 square meters, and 30% of it is reclaimed land, including its airport and its recreational island, Sentosa; that, even though Singapore is smaller than Hong Kong, it's doing pretty well; and that, because Singapore can't get any bigger, in 2006 Malaysia saw an opportunity to claim some of Singapore's business growth.

The Smiling Salesman's laser pointer circled, focusing in on the different zones of Iskandar: Zone E holds the Johor International Airport; Zone A is the old city center where the first bridge to Singapore was built, but it was outdated and not well planned in the first place; Zone B is considered the new city center; and Forest City is the island to the south of the entire zone.

There are seven universities here, the Smiling Salesman went on, and all are ranked in the top 200 globally. He told me that education used to be better in Singapore, and Malaysia used to have no schools, but now some of the British universities have opened campuses there—including the Marlborough School's Asian campus, where Kate Middleton studied. Since these institutions have relocated, many Singaporeans are settling in Malaysia.

Zone B is also a cultural zone, and Malaysia is proud to have the first Lego Land in Asia, as well as the new Pinewood Iskandar Malaysia studios, a Hollywood film studio that is already turning a profit. Zone B is also where the hospitals are located. Because everything in Malaysia is about 60% cheaper than in Singapore, more and more people are coming to take care of their medical needs. The Gleneagles Medini Hospital has the ability to do anything that the one in Singapore can do, but cheaper.

The Smiling Salesman looked at me and said, "For the price of one property in Singapore, you can buy seven in Forest City. And there is no tax here *and* it's *FREEHOLD*. In Singapore, you can only have a 99-year lease on your property. It is *FREEHOLD* in Malaysia."

The Smiling Salesman's laser pointer circled around one cluster of apartments. "Those apartments are Phase 1, and those are Phase 2. They're sold out." He points to another cluster, "Those are Phase 3, and they are available for you."

As my tour continued, Mr. Aw and the Smiling Salesman walked me through the community and shopping areas. Directly outside was a cluster of landscaped swimming pools where families were enjoying the water and taking selfies. I could see Singapore from the pools which overlooked the Johor Strait. Many children were splashing around with their parents and their parents' parents—a picture of the multigenerational demographic Forest City seemed to desire.

We headed indoors to another side of the glass building, which featured the model units. There were options: a studio apartment, one-bedroom, two-bedroom, and three-bedroom. All were similarly and tastefully decorated, with distinct color palettes and a nice balance of textures. Living rooms had a leather sofa in light brown or light grey, a mid-century inspired coffee table, maybe a porcelain tea set, some coffee table books on home decor, a leather ottoman, a linen armchair, an earth-toned striped rug. The kitchens all seemed designed for families or couples—no one lived alone in Forest City. There were bowls of plastic fruit, plates of carved-foam cake, varieties of olive oil, and champagne for two. The dining table could be set for four or six, and all of the chairs were big, upholstered, and heavy. The bedrooms had plenty of storage space—walk-in closets, wood armoires, and shelves lined with picture frames of sample family moments: a child on a swing, a wedding, and a father and son fishing in a small boat. The beds were piled with decorative pillows, and one displayed a swan folded out of a towel. Kids' rooms were outfitted with bunk beds, desks, stuffed animals, toy trucks, dolls, and an alphabet board. Bathrooms were marble and glass, and master baths had tubs with jets.

As I stepped out onto a model balcony, I was greeted by a grilling station, complete with plastic skewers and some plastic plants made to look like they were growing off of the balcony.

I turned to the Smiling Salesman and asked him, "How many varieties of plants will be grown in Forest City, and what are they?" "Many kinds!" he replied. "What kinds?" I asked again. He said he would get back to me. All day I had been looking at tangled and coiled plastic plants, and a few real plants of the tropical-resort variety. Of the plastic plants, I could count maybe five different shapes; and of the real ones, I counted palm trees, bromeliads, chestnut trees, and a handful of other short shrubs and flowers. I did not see close to 100 species of plants, as the newspapers had reported.

Leaving the model units, I was fixated on the art on one living room's wall. I had seen a few similar pieces throughout the day, but this particular one was probably seven feet tall and hung behind a TV screen that was playing a Forest City promotional video on a loop. It was a giant photographic print of an autumn landscape in the Northern US. In the foreground were some thick pine branches. In the distance were enormous grey-blue mountains with snow caps. Clouds sailed across the peaceful blue sky. There was a line of birch trees with golden yellow leaves. The whole top part of the landscape was reflected in a crystal clear body of water that extended all the way down to the print's bottom edge. It was a picture of another paradise, but not of the King Kong or Jurassic Park variety. This paradise was not anywhere close to Malaysia, and yet whatever the picture seemed to mean in terms of aspirations and success, it made sense here in this living room in the middle of a man-made tropic.

A dental implant is made of three parts: the body, the abutment, and the crown. The body is a hollow titanium cylinder that most resembles a screw. It goes up against the gums in the clear spot between the two adjacent teeth. Six to eight months after the body is installed, the surgeon cuts back into the gums and twists in abutment holders, which look like metal nubs. This is what is visible while the crowns are being made, which takes about three weeks. Finally, the crowns are fitted: the nubs are removed and replaced with abutments, which are also titanium with a screw body, but which have angled, pointy heads that get cemented to the crown.

A few weeks before the day for phase one of my surgery, my teeth were scrubbed down, like when my braces were taken off. Dr. Fujishige's assistant snapped off the tooth-colored plastic attachments, the plaque was chipped away with a pointed tool, pumice swished around with an electric brush, and a special whitening medium was sprayed all over my teeth with a cold air tube. By the end of it all, my teeth felt like smooth marble as I ran my tongue across them. I was ready.

Dr. Chen greeted me and then picked up a long Q-tip that had been soaking in a numbing gel. Within a few minutes, I was only half in the room. I could see what was going on, could even feel Dr. Chen touching my mouth, but everything felt gentle. Then there were two slight punctures through my gums on the right and left gaps. "And you're done," said Dr. Chen. Not even 20 minutes had passed, and he had already sewn up my gums, now with new biocompatible parts inside.

After surgery, Dr. Chen's nurses took me to a dark resting area, seated me in an armchair, and wrapped me in a soft throw. I was surprised that I was not in pain. My gums were swollen, and it was a little awkward to eat, but not so much that I needed special food. The only issue was that my prosthetic teeth did not fit. I didn't go anywhere too public for the next few weeks, until my gums slowly shrank and I was able to squeeze my prosthetic in and resume life as normal.

At the end of my tour, Mr. Aw offered to drop me off at the hotel, just over the bridge on mainland Johor. "It is a five-star gold resort overlooking our new eighteen-hole golf course," he told me on the drive over.

We passed by piles of dirt until we reached the grand, looping entrance to the resort. Unlike the Forest City building, this building was mostly made of dark wood. The lobby ceiling was so high that there was enough space for the BMW 520d parked in the center of the room to sit beneath a giant gold sculpture that hung from the ceiling. "Everything is complimentary. Keep in touch, and tell your husband to come next time!" Mr. Aw said goodbye with a smile.

There was hardly anyone at this resort, except for the group of Hà-Nội-an ladies I had seen earlier at lunch. Now, they were lounging in bathrobes and enjoying the buffet dinner, which featured a spectrum of international foods: coconut curry smothered shrimp, strip steak, iceberg lettuce, noodles. There was also an eclectic dessert bar, with delicate cubes of tiramisu, blueberry cream cake, lemon curd, and fudge. I ate alone and went up to my room.

The room was enormous. There was a giant king-size bed covered with orange decorative pillows. I had a balcony that overlooked the sprawling golf-course, which was deserted. All I could see was one small crane in the far distance. The sun was quickly setting, and the grass on the golf course was no longer visible. All I could see was the light from that faraway crane, which now looked a little bit like a star. "David Van would have loved this place," I thought to myself.

While it takes six to eight months for an implant to become part of any human body, it took me almost a year to complete the implant process. This was mostly because I needed to find a block of days in which I could heal without anyone seeing me in process—a day when Dr. Chen could uncover my implants in the morning and I could see Dr. Fujishige immediately after so he could adjust my prosthetic. This special day was a challenge to find, but eventually we found it: June 14, 2019.

I went to Dr. Chen's office for a short final visit. He took some x-rays, which were projected for me in a consultation room. Dr. Chen waltzed in and, within a few seconds of looking at the screen, exclaimed, "Yes! That looks good!" He turned to me, held my chin and told me to open my mouth. "Looks good," he said again. After he saw that I had healed well and that my body had accepted the implants, he proceeded to open my gums.

Just as in the first surgery, Dr. Chen dabbed some numbing gel onto my gums. I could feel small prickling sensations, and then he was done. When I looked into the mirror, I could see there were round shiny metal nubs sticking out from my gums. It looked clean, but a little horrifying, evoking Frankenstein or other sci-fi imaginings. I felt clear-headed. I took the B train downtown to Dr. Fujishige's office.

I was mainly concerned with how I would get my prosthetic to cover these metal nubs for the next three weeks. Dr. Fujishige shaved down the plastic and the false teeth to fit around my new metal nubs. Then he made a 3D scan of my mouth and a plaster impression, along with several digital photos, all for the dental artisan who would sculpt my permanent crowns from zirconia, a ceramic material that is generally found in placer deposits—deposits of wind-worked sand on riverbeds, much like the sand left behind by the millions of years of wind that carved away at Phong Nha.

Three weeks later, my crowns were ready. The tiny little things were waiting for me in a black jewelry box in Dr. Fujishige's consultation room. "Okay, let's see if this works. They have to be perfect!" he said with his usual cheer. He used a tiny screwdriver to remove the metal nubs from the tubular body of the implant. There was a smell of deep body buildup so foul that it made me think of death, perhaps how David Van must have smelled when they found his body rotting alone in his house.

"Your crowns will sit 0.5 mm below your gums," Dr. Fujishige explained as he twisted two pointy abutments into the body of the implant. "We are going to use a special cement that is really going to make these crowns stick to the abutment." He squeezed out a gooey substance. In a few minutes, the whole thing was done, the life saga complete. The entire office's staff rushed in. "They look real!" everyone exclaimed.

Real enough, but I can still feel the difference. There is virtually no sensation in my gums where my false teeth are. When I bite onto them, I feel only a toughness. Not like my natural teeth, which can feel everything that enters my mouth.

The total cost of correcting my birth defect, including my childhood braces, was nearly $20,000. In the end, insurance covered $1,200 because Dr. Fujishige's office argued that my condition was congenital. I thought about this a month later, when I found myself swimming through one of the caves in the Phong Nha Karst. As I swam, the passageway became narrower. I had to listen for the sound of water trickling to find my way out. I opened my mouth and blew some O's into the water, and let some of it run through my teeth. As the water pushed through, the cold isolated itself on my front teeth, charging my brain with a freezing sensation. But the implants on either side just sat, firm and unmoved.

Socrates told his young disciple Glaucon to imagine a vertical line. "Now divide it in half," he continued. Glaucon nodded, and Socrates said, "Now divide those two sections in half." Glaucon did as Socrates said.

"There are two realms. The visible, which exists under the line, below the intelligible realm. The lowest form of truth lies in the first section of the divided line. Let's call this *imagination*. These are things such as shadows and illusion."

Glaucon nodded, attentive.

"Moving up the line, the second section, which is a higher truth than *imagination*, is *belief*. That's the world of physical objects—literally, what is around us, Glaucon, the fabric that covers our bodies, that tree over there, this vessel of water."

Glaucon continued looking at Socrates, nodding in acceptance.

"Now, we will move over the dividing line into the intelligible realm. Take a triangle that is equal on all sides. You know that such a triangle exists without actually seeing it. This is what we could call the realm of *reason*."

Glaucon quietly repeated everything Socrates said and then nodded in acknowledgement.

"Moving up to a higher truth, we reach the realm of *nous*, or *knowledge*: *intellect*. This is when reason transcends itself, becoming a form. Let's say, for example, I take this vessel and I pour the water out of it. Well, the water spills out because of gravity. This is a truth that humans know, not because it was an instinct, but because it was discovered through intelligible discovery and critical thinking. Or, let's look at that mountain over there. It's beautiful, isn't it? How do you know it's beautiful? Is there a greater truth of beauty, one that could be discovered through a process of thinking? Possibly, and this truth would be a form that transcends space and time. If the earth were to end, the truth of beauty would not need the earth to still be true."

Glaucon looked over at the mountains. They had round, amiable peaks, with a dense forest that blanketed them in curls of green flora.

"But what do you need to understand all of this, Glaucon?"

Glaucon continued to look at the mountains. Like a grand driveway, or a gigantic lawn to mark the importance of a place, these mountains were surrounded with miles of rice paddies. Perhaps it was the time of year, but these rice paddies glistened with an electric green, the kind you might see at a nightclub or painted on a Lamborghini. It was strange to see such green in nature.

"Light, Glaucon, you need light. Truth is only possible because of the sun."

Glaucon turned back to look at Socrates.

"Let me tell you a story. In an ancient time, three prisoners were chained inside a cave in such a way that they could only stare at the cave's wall. There was a fire burning behind them, and behind that fire was the cave's opening. Over centuries, things would pass by and cast shadows onto the cave's wall. There was a big mound that would usually appear at the center of the wall. Triangles with other shapes stacked on top would circle the mound. One prisoner called these shapes boats, and the other decided to call the mound *Island*. Other times, when the mound would disappear, the prisoners would see a moving form constantly pulling rectangular forms from inside of it and giving them to other moving forms. They named the giving form David Van, and the rectangles they called money. David Van would come and go on the days when they could not see the mound. Once, David Van had so many rectangles that the other forms stacked the rectangles on top of each other and the prisoners called the giant rectangle house. There was also a strange day when a giant shape rose out of the mound. They named this form King Kong."

Socrates continued: "The only thing the prisoners could see were these shadows. The prisoners would play a game with each other, guessing what shadow would pass on the wall next. Whoever guessed correctly would receive praise from the others and be deemed the 'Master of Nature.'"

But one day, a prisoner broke free and turned around. The fire that had been burning behind him was hot and orange, a color more intense than the orange he had been staring at on the wall. He walked closer to the fire, but the heat started to make his skin sting. When the fire burnt him, he jumped away and looked up."

Glaucon leaned in, intrigued.

"When the prisoner looked up, he saw a long tube, something that reminded him of his own throat. Swallowing his own breath and spit, he gaped at the steep passage spanning hundreds of meters. It was filled with stalactites and stalagmites, protruding like overgrown teeth. He started to climb. For the most part, his movements upwards were triangular: left leg on a rock to the left, hands reaching at a point overhead, right leg following at an angled point to the right. And just like that, he made a steady course upwards and over."

Glaucon moved his fingers on his thigh as if to mimic the prisoner's triangular movement.

"Now, Glaucon, as I continue this story, I want you to remember that this big tube the prisoner is climbing up is precisely the divided line I had told you about. And the higher he climbs, the closer he comes to truth—to *the good*, which is the highest level of wisdom and knowledge."

Glaucon nodded, and Socrates continued.

"As he climbed to brighter patches of rock, he started to see that plants were growing. He climbed higher and the plants became longer and more prominent, many of them showing off large leaves. He could see that the bright round disc was not a disc, but a portal. At the highest rock, a blue butterfly flew in from the other side of the portal and rested on a leaf."

Glaucon sat up straight and slightly lifted his head, sensing a change in the story's direction.

"The prisoner finally came to the plane of the portal and stumbled through. The light was unlike anything he had experienced before. He squinted his eyes so his eyelashes could break the light, and he veiled his face with his hand. While his sight was a blur, his ears were alert to the noisy surroundings. He heard water splashing, children laughing, and footsteps shuffling around. As the light started to settle in his eyes, he took his hand from his face and, in the near distance, saw an enormous mountain. No one was near it; it loomed over the earth, rising so high that it almost touched this even brighter light that was floating in the sky."

Glaucon started to smile, as he knew what the brighter light was.

"The prisoner looked around and saw that there were long lounge chairs and tables scattered around the area. The splashing water was coming from a string of swimming pools, and the children were laughing as they ran from one pool to the next. They leaped into the sky and landed in the water like big, friendly explosions. One pool had a tube, a little bit like the one he had just come out of, but it was yellow and smooth, and children could climb to the top and slide down back into the water."

Glaucon was a little perplexed as to where Socrates was going.

"As the prisoner watched the children, he noticed that each child had a shape similar to their body, which moved with them as they ran from pool to pool. He looked around and noticed that almost everything had a darker shape beneath it. A chair and a long table both had dark shapes beneath them, and these shapes shared outlines that were angled in parallel. The prisoner saw that the table was decadently covered in food. On its right side, he saw giant prawns drenched in a coconut peanut sauce, sautéed cabbage, pasta with sauces, curry stewed chicken, stir-fried beef, rice, a variety of pickled vegetables, and a fountain of Sprite. On its left, he saw coconut curry smothered shrimp, strip steak, iceberg lettuce, and noodles. Farther down the table, he saw cubes of tiramisu, blueberry cream cake, lemon curd, and fudge. As he approached the food, he could see a dark shape cast over it that moved with him as he sniffed and examined each dish. He looked back up at the mountain, and now he could look directly at the bright light above it."

Glaucon's mouth was salivating and his body was tense with excitement as Socrates continued.

"The prisoner realized that the bright light was creating the dark shapes. As he moved with his own dark shape, he noticed that he could only see the shapes when the bright light was behind him. He looked at the big mountain and then back at the cave's mouth, where he'd come from. 'It is not an *Island,* but a *Mountain,*' he thought to himself. Satisfied with his new knowledge—his new truth—he started to devour the food on the table. It was the most pleasure he had felt in a long time. The curry sauce gushed around his mouth, blueberries squished underneath his tongue, and he gnawed the steak off its T-bone. Then he heard a high-pitched cry: *'MAMA! SHE HAS NO TEETH!'*"

Glaucon's eyes widened in disbelief.

"Startled, the prisoner dropped his food and ran back into the hole, tripping, falling all the way down. When he landed on the dark floor, he found that he could no longer see the shadows, or his friends, clearly. Grabbing their legs for support, he tried to explain. 'Friends, it is not an *Island,* but a *Mountain*!' One of the other prisoners replied, 'What is it you're saying? What is a *Mountain*? *That* is the *Island*. Challenge us again and we will kill you.'"

Glaucon sat back, a little disappointed.

"And so, the prisoner wandered off to a dark corner of the cave where he could see nothing at all, not the flickering of the fire or the rays of the sun. Seated on the floor with his head between his knees, he started to let out a wail, 'O-O-O-O-O-O-O.' Meanwhile, outside the cave, the children splashed around, laughing. As the adults continued to lounge and eat, they would hear a sound coming from the cave: 'O-O-O-O-O-O-O.' They would stop for a second. Elders would whisper to each other, 'There are ghosts in that cave.' Parents would hold their children and say, 'Don't go in there, there are ghosts in that cave.' And so life went on. Everyone continued to enjoy the swimming pools and food beside the mountain, never ever going into the cave."

FINIS.

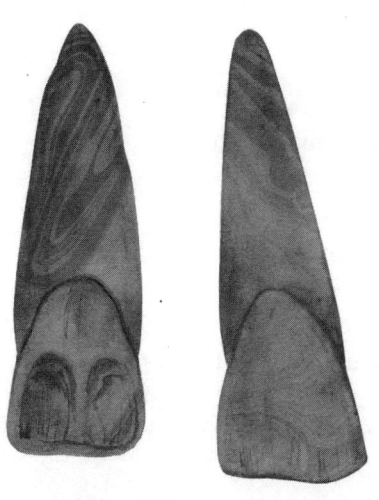

Phong Nha, the Making of an American Smile
© Tammy Nguyễn, 2020

2020 Pamphlet Series
ISBN 978-1-946433-41-1
First Edition, First Printing
Edition of 1,000

Ugly Duckling Presse
The Old American Can Factory
232 Third Street, #E-303
Brooklyn, NY 11215
uglyducklingpresse.org

Distributed in the USA by SPD/Small Press Distribution
Distributed in the UK by Inpress

Series design by chuck kuan and Sarah Lawson
Typeset by Don't Look Now!
Type is New Century Schoolbook and TeX Gyre Schola
Cover and flyleaf from French Paper Co.
Printed offset and bound at McNaughton & Gunn
Flyleaf printed letterpress at Ugly Duckling Presse

This publication was made possible by a grant from the New York City Department of Cultural Affairs, and by the support of the New York State Council on the Arts, a state agency.

This pamphlet is part of UDP's 2020 Pamphlet Series: twenty commissioned essays on poetics, translation, performance, collective work, pedagogy, and small press publishing. The authors are listed below; their pamphlets are available for individual purchase and as a subscription (uglyducklingpresse.org/subscribe). Each offers a different approach to the pamphlet as a form of working in the present, an engagement at once sustained and ephemeral.

Mirene Arsanios
Omar Berrada
Sergio Chejfec
Don Mee Choi
Kunci Study Forum & Collective
Iris Cushing
Simon Cutts
Nicole Cecilia Delgado
Adjua Gargi Nzinga Greaves
Dimitra Ioannou

Sibyl Kempson
Claudia La Rocco
Aditi Machado
Chantal Maillard
Tinashe Mushakavanhu
Sawako Nakayasu
Tammy Nguyen
Aleksandr Skidan
Steven Zultanski
Magdalena Zurawski

To win a subscription, write to office@uglyducklingpresse.org with your solution to the following puzzle: Using only 6 straight lines, divide the circle on the back cover so that each number is in its own section, without any overlap between numbers.